Explore the Outdoors

Bike Trekking

Have Fun, Be Smart

by Chris Hayhurst

Published in 2000 by The Rosen Publishing Group, Inc.
29 East 21st Street, New York, NY 10010

First Edition

Hayhurst, Chris.
   Bike trekking : have fun, be smart / by Chris Hayhurst.
     p. cm.— (Explore the outdoors)
   Includes bibliographical references and index.
   Summary: This book describes the sport of bike trekking, the equipment and gear needed, the techniques of biking, and the safety precautions.
   ISBN 0-8239-3172-2
   1. Cycling—Juvenile literature. 2. Bicycle touring—Juvenile literature. [1. Bicycles and bicycling.] I. Title. II. Series.
   2000
   796.6—dc21

Manufactured in the United States of America

Contents

Introduction

Have you ever dreamed you could go anywhere in the world? Have you ever imagined what it would be like to be absolutely free? Of course you have; everyone does. That's one of the biggest reasons people travel—to get away, to see new places, to experience life in a different pair of shoes.

One of the best ways to travel is by bicycle. The bike allows you to ride to places that you otherwise would have to drive or walk to. You can ride your bike to school or just use it to zip around the neighborhood. If you've got a mountain bike, you can use it on trails. You can jump with it or race with it. If you are in the mood, you can just cruise.

One thing many people don't realize is that a bicycle can also be used to travel to distant places. A bike gives you the freedom to visit places that are too far away to reach on foot—not just the grocery store or the movie theater but really far away places. If you've got the legs and the know-how, you can pedal your bike just about anywhere. Want to see the other side of the state? Your bike can take you there. Contemplating a trip across the country? Hop aboard your bike. Dreaming about Tibet, Tasmania, or Timbuktu? All it takes—well, almost all it takes—is two wheels.

With two wheels, two legs, and a good set of lungs, you can use your bike to do things you've never dreamed of and to see things you never thought you would ever get to see. The fact is, your bike—and the sport of bike trekking—gives you a wonderful way to witness the world.

But bike trekking isn't as simple as that. You can't really just hop on your bike and go. You have to make sure you know what you are doing first. Will your bike hold up under long miles on the road? Is it tuned up and in good working condition? Are you in good shape, and do you know what it takes to pedal beyond—way beyond—the driveway? Most important, do you know how to trek safely? You have to know the rules of the road. Although incredibly exciting and rewarding, bike trekking can also be a very dangerous sport. And getting hurt is no fun at all.

Before you jump in the saddle and pedal to Peru, read this book to learn what bike trekking is all about. By the time you're through, you just might have what it takes to explore the world by bike.

1 Getting Started

If you've never gone on a multi-day bicycle tour, the idea of pedaling off into the sunset may sound like a major challenge. But the fact is, getting started in bicycle trekking is easy. You just have to know what to expect down the road.

Before you run out and buy all the gear—a bike, panniers, tools, and camping equipment—take a step back and make sure bicycle trekking is for you. This sport is not for couch potatoes. You have to enjoy working to get from place to place. You also have to love the outdoors and everything that comes with it, like bad weather and steep hills. Sound inviting? Then step right up.

If you already have a bike, you are well on your way to getting started. Just about any bike will do as long as it is strong, tuned up, and fits you. If you don't have a bike, you should be able to pick up a used one through the want ads or the Internet, or you can find a new one at your local bike store. The salespeople at bike stores can usually help you find exactly what bike will fit you and your needs best.

Once you have a bike, it is time to look into the rest of the gear. Again, shop around. Buying used equipment is often a smart move, especially if you're not 100 percent sure trekking is for you. If you have a friend who has toured before, ask him or

her questions you have about gear. A friend's input on what works best can save you a lot of time and money.

OK. You've got the gear and the desire. Are you ready to ride? Are you in shape? Can you handle all the miles of pedaling up and down hills with a loaded bike? A good way to answer these questions is by going on a few short practice rides. If you're planning to go on a long trip in a month or two, get out and do several shorter day trips first. Load up your panniers with the things that you will bring on your extended trip, and get a feel for what it is like to pedal all day long weighted down with gear. You can learn a lot on short rides like these.

If you don't have a lot of time before your first multi-day trek, never fear. On long trips—those of at least a week—

> *Bicycling is a very popular sport. More than 48 million people in the United States ride bikes every year!*

you'll get in shape naturally as you go. The first few days may seem difficult, but eventually your leg muscles will kick in and the miles will become easier.

The most important thing to realize about getting started in bicycle trekking—or any sport for that matter—is that you will get better over time. As life on the bike becomes more familiar, it also gets easier. No one is a born expert in anything—so just get out there and have fun!

Types and Styles of Trekking

There are many different ways to trek by bicycle. In fact, you could say that every person treks in his or her own way—in his or her own direction and pace, and with individual ideas of what to see and do.

Want to ride your bike from Anchorage, Alaska, to Miami, Florida? Or from Portland, Maine, to San Diego, California? How about a shorter trip? Perhaps a trek across your home state or just across your county. Or maybe you are in the mood for something really grand, like a tour down Mexico's Baja Peninsula or a journey around the world.

Where you want to ride often determines the type or style of bicycle trekking required to get there. Trek across the remote desert outback of Australia, for instance, and you will

Family Fun

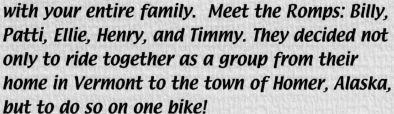

It's one thing to ride a bike from Vermont to Alaska, but it's another thing to make the six-month-long trip with your entire family. Meet the Romps: Billy, Patti, Ellie, Henry, and Timmy. They decided not only to ride together as a group from their home in Vermont to the town of Homer, Alaska, but to do so on one bike!

One bike for five people? Well, almost. The bike actually seats four. The fifth person—in the Romp family's case, three-year-old Timmy—is towed in a two-wheel trailer.

probably need a support van to carry your food and water. Ride 100 miles from your house to the beach and back and you can probably carry everything you need for the two- or three-day trip.

How fit are you? How much experience do you have? If you are in great shape, you probably won't need a sag wagon—a car or van that rides along to provide support—and you shouldn't have any trouble schlepping all your gear yourself. Likewise, if you are an experienced camper, pitching a tent may seem more inviting than spending a night in a hostel or motel room. But if you have never been on a trek before and can't set up a campsite to save your life, you may be better off making your first journey with a group under the leadership of a professional guide who can teach you all the necessary skills. If you have no experience at all, it is unwise to set out on a solo journey around the globe.

A self-contained bike tour is one in which the riders carry everything they need to get from start to finish. They stuff sleeping bags and tents into their panniers, have flashlights and maps within reach, and pack enough food and water to ensure that they won't go hungry. A fully supported trip, on the other hand, is one in which the riders carry nothing but themselves on their bikes. A sag wagon, carrying everyone's gear, accompanies the riders from place to place. Many trips fall between these two extremes, with riders using a support vehicle for some of the distance, or stopping at motel rooms instead of backcountry campsites.

Another decision bike trekkers must make is whether to ride off-road or on-road. Some bikers prefer to ride trails instead of paved country roads and highways. Others would rather stick to the roads, where the riding is smooth and fast, and where help, if it's needed, is only a car away. Trails usually require a mountain bike, whereas maintained highways are sometimes better traveled on a road bike.

Whatever style of bicycle trekking you choose, make sure you plan your trip carefully. Don't wait until you are fifty miles into a trip to find that you can't continue unless you swap your road bike for a mountain bike. And don't pull into camp on your first night expecting a cozy room and a fancy meal. Just know where you are going and how you are going to get there, and before you shift into gear you will be well on your way to the perfect trip.

2 Equipment

One of the most complicated things about traveling by bicycle is fitting the gear you need into the space you have to bring it. In other words, you must pack carefully.

Of course, the main piece of equipment you will need is a bike. The bike is your vehicle, your home, and your suitcase all rolled into one.

Good touring bikes take many shapes and sizes, but all have one thing in common: durability. They have to be strong. Today many cyclists use mountain bikes, which have fat wheels, beefy frames, and a compact size. They can handle a variety of different riding conditions—from trails to rugged dirt roads to paved highways. Others swear by the classic touring bike, which has a larger frame, fenders, and dropped handlebars. Whether you choose to ride a mountain bike, a road bike, or one that's somewhere in between is up to you.

Bike Basics

The bike is quite a piece of machinery. To have fun and stay safe while bike trekking, you need to have at least a minimum understanding of how your bicycle works. Here's a list of things you may find on yours:

Bottom bracket: This is where your cranks are attached to the bike. The cranks are enabled to spin thanks to the bottom-bracket bearing, which is held in the bottom-bracket shell.

Brakes: You do need to slow down once in a while.

Chain-rings: The three cogs, smallest on the inside and largest on the outside, fitted to the chain set. The chain fits over a chain-ring's teeth.

Chain set: The complete set of crank, chain-rings, and bottom bracket.

Mountain Bike

Chain stay: The two bottom frame tubes that run from the bottom-bracket shell to the hub of the rear wheel.

Cranks: The two metal arms on either side of the bike that run from the pedals to the bottom-bracket axle.

Derailleurs: There are two: front and rear. They move the chain when you shift gears.

Fork: The fork holds the front wheel and houses the steerer tube.

Freewheel: This allows the rear wheel to keep rolling when you stop pedaling.

Handlebars: Use them to steer. This is where your grips and brake levers are mounted. If you have a mountain bike, your shifters will be up here, too.

Headset: This houses the bearings that allow the steerer tube to rotate. It is located right above the top-front point of the frame.

Hub: There are two hubs, one at the center of each wheel. They support the spokes and hold the ball bearings that enable the wheels to spin smoothly.

Pedals: Most pedals are now clipless, meaning there are no straps, just metal cleats to which your shoes attach.

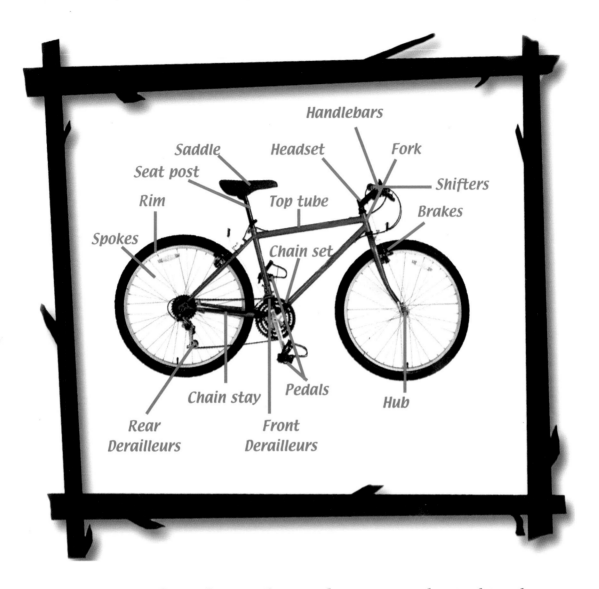

Handlebars

Saddle   Headset   Fork

Seat post

Shifters

Rim   Top tube

Brakes

Spokes

Chain set

Chain stay   Pedals

Hub

Rear
Derailleurs

Front
Derailleurs

Presta/Schrader valves: The Presta valve is thin, the Schrader is thick. Make sure you have a pump that fits your valve.

Quick releases: These devices allow you to quickly tighten or loosen your seat post and wheels.

Rims: The two metal hoops on which the tubes and tires are mounted.

Saddle: Another word for a bike seat.

Seat post: The tube to which the seat is attached.

Shifters: Mechanisms mounted on the handlebars or on the bike frame that allow you to change gears.

Spokes: The thin metal cables that connect a wheel's hub to the rim.

Top tube: The horizontal top part of the frame that runs from the headset to the seat post.

Most of what the bike trekker carries is packed into sturdy bags called panniers. Panniers attach to metal racks that are fastened to the bike's frame. If you find that your panniers just aren't big enough to hold everything you need, you can strap your extra stuff to the rear rack, which sits conveniently right behind the bike seat, over the rear wheel. Finally, you can mount a small bag on your handlebars and fill it with items you may need on the road, like your sunglasses, maps, and money. If you pack for an extended, self-contained trip, one where it is just you, the road, and your gear, your rig may end up looking more like a tank than a bike.

How you pack your bike depends on how long you plan to ride, whether there will be towns every few miles or only every few days, and where you plan to stay. It also depends on the weather—if you ride in the winter in New England, for instance, you had better be ready for the cold.

If you will be camping along your route, you need to

pack the appropriate camping gear. Make sure you divide the big things—like the tent, stove, and cook set—among all the riders in your group. That way one person won't be stuck carrying all of the weight. If you ride alone, you had better pack light or be very strong!

If you will be staying in youth hostels or other accommodations that provide a kitchen and a place to sleep, your load will be much lighter. Things like a sleeping bag, tent, and pad can be left at home. Likewise, if there are many towns along your route, you can generally carry less food and stop at local stores to pick up whatever you need along the way.

The key to an enjoyable trek is packing everything you need while paying attention to the details, like weight. You don't have to trim ounces, but you should watch the pounds. When you're faced with a very steep hill at the end of the day, you will be happy that you left the heavy things behind.

Packing

What to bring on a bike trip is up to you. There are a few things that you should bring, however. Below and on the next few pages are lists of necessities to get you started.

You will also need to pack whatever toiletries you regularly use, such as your toothbrush and toothpaste. And don't forget the little extras—the things that might take up space

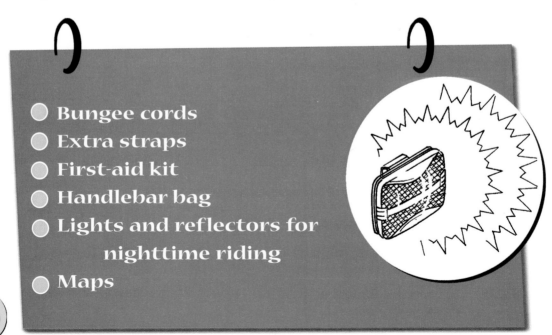

- Bungee cords
- Extra straps
- First-aid kit
- Handlebar bag
- Lights and reflectors for nighttime riding
- Maps

- Money
- Panniers (front and rear)
- Plastic bags
- Pocketknife
- Sunscreen
- Tool kit
- Water bottles
- Water purification system

Camping Equipment

- Cookstove
- Cooking set
  (pan, pot, bowl, mug, utensils)
- Flashlight
- Fuel bottle/extra fuel
- Ground cloth
- Matches/lighter
- Pack towel (chamois)
- Sleeping bag
- Sleeping pad
- Tent

but that will make you happy when the going gets tough, like a book, camera, journal, or playing cards.

What to Wear

Light; easy to wash; easy to dry. Keep these three qualities in mind when you are choosing your cycling wardrobe and you will be ready for anything.

Cotton Kills

Cotton may be comfortable when it is dry, but when it is wet the fabric can be downright dangerous. Cotton tends to

- ○ **Bandanna**
- ○ **Baseball cap**
- ○ **Casual clothes** (pack sparingly)
- ○ **Cycling gloves** (they prevent blisters and provide protection in the event that you fall)
- ○ **Cycling shoes** (the soles of bike shoes are stiffer than those of regular shoes; inset cleats allow you to use clipless pedals, which in turn permit more efficient pedaling)
- ○ **Cycling shorts** (they look like regular athletic shorts with pockets but have built-in synthetic padding designed to prevent saddle sores and chafing)
- ○ **Cycling socks** (two pairs)
- ○ **Cycling tights**
- ○ **Fleece and polypropylene top and bottom**

- ○ **Fleece hat**
- ○ **Fleece sweater**
- ○ **Helmet**
- ○ **Long-sleeve polypropylene top**
- ○ **Sandals or running shoes**
- ○ **Shorts** (can double as swimsuit for guys)
- ○ **Short-sleeve polypropylene jersey** (plus one extra for extended trips; pockets allow you to stash things)
- ○ **Sunglasses** (they make you look cool while protecting your eyes from ultraviolet rays and allowing you to see better)
- ○ **Swimsuit**
- ○ **T-shirt** (polypropylene)
- ○ **Underwear**
- **Waterproof jacket and pants**

absorb moisture—like sweat or rain—and hold it against your body. That is exactly what you don't want to happen when you are biking. Just add a cool breeze and before you know it you will be shivering from head to toe. You could get hypothermia—a potentially life-threatening condition in which your body temperature drops to an unsafe level. So when you are trying to decide what to wear on a bike trip, avoid cotton whenever possible and instead wear clothing made from synthetic materials such as polypropylene or fleece. Unlike cotton, these fabrics wick moisture away from your skin, so sweat never even has a chance to cool you down.

- **Adjustable wrench**
- **Allen keys**
- **Chain tool**
- **Crank-arm wrench** (make sure you buy the right type and size for your crank)
- **Crescent wrench**
  - **Extra nuts and bolts**
    - **Freewheel tool**
      - **Liquid lubricant**
        - **Patch kit**
        - **Pedal wrench**
        - **Pliers**
        - **Pump**
        - **Screwdrivers** (flat-blade and Phillips-head)
    - **Spare chain links**
  - **Spare spokes** (tape to the chain stay), cables (brake and derailleur), brake shoes
- **Spare tire**
- **Spare tube**
- **Spoke wrench**
- **Tire irons**

Touring Tools

It helps to be a mechanic when you go on extended touring trips. Your bike can break down anywhere—and will usually do so a long way from the nearest shop. Pack the bike tools and spare parts listed on the previous page every time you go on a ride and you'll be able to work your way out of almost any problem short of a broken frame. Just make sure you know how to use everything before you go!

To Clip or Not to Clip

There are few components on your bike more important than your pedals—without them you would go nowhere. Although most pedals pretty much look the same, the fact is there are many different kinds. The biggest difference between pedals is how they fasten to your feet.

Some pedals come with straps and plastic or metal toe cups. You place your foot on the pedal, snug your toes into the toe cup, and cinch down the straps until your foot is held tightly in place. By securing your foot to the pedal, you can pull up as well as push down with every stroke.

clipless

Other pedals are called clipless (even though you do clip in to them) and eliminate the need for straps. Like ski bindings, they allow you to attach the sole of your shoe directly to a metal mechanism on the pedal. With a mere twist of your foot, you can clip in or out with ease. These pedals also allow you to push and pull, and are very popular among serious cyclists.

So which style should you use? Try both types of pedals, talk to the salesperson at your local bike shop, and pick the best style for you.

3 Technique

Unlike many sports, bicycle trekking doesn't require a lot of specialized techniques. If you know how to ride a bike, are in reasonably good shape, and have a desire to see the world from the seat of your rig, you pretty much have what it takes to be a touring cyclist.

You do need to know how to take care of yourself and your bike, however. For example, you never know when your bike is going to break down. If you are more than a few miles from the nearest bike shop and your chain breaks, for instance, you had better know how to use your chain tool to fix it. And you had better know how to take care of minor injuries. It is not uncommon to take a fall and end up with a few scrapes and bruises. If you don't have a first-aid kit or don't know how to use what is in it, you may be in trouble.

It also helps to have a few camping skills up your sleeve. Camping with your bike is similar to camping with a backpack: You carry everything you need with you, but if you don't know how to use it all it won't do you any good. Before you hit the road, make sure you know how to set up your tent, operate your cookstove, and keep an orderly camp. If you are cycling and a sudden storm rolls in, you will be glad you've got your camping skills wired.

As far as the actual riding goes, the main technique you should master is how to conserve energy. This means finding a pace that you and your riding partners are comfortable with and taking regular breaks for food and water to ensure that you don't bonk (run out of energy or otherwise find yourself unable to continue). In any group, some riders will be stronger than others. Ride at a pace that you all can enjoy.

You can also conserve energy by learning how to pedal efficiently. Good pedaling technique—the kind of pedaling that lets you continue at the same pace for hours—comes with lots of practice. When you know how to "spin" your wheels, or pedal in circles by both pulling up and pushing down with each crank revolution, you will find that the hills become a lot easier and the flats a lot faster. In the end you will cover many more

miles while expending much less energy.

An entire book could be written about how to draft (riding in a line to reduce wind-resistance), how to distribute the weight of your gear on your bike, how to get in touring shape, and how to climb, descend, and ultimately conquer the road. But the one thing most people never consider is motivation. If you're having trouble staying motivated during your tour, the days will seem endless and your body will become ragged. Always keep your goals in sight. If you know why you are on a tour in the first place and think it feels good to work your legs day in and day out, you will never get bored and you will find new things to keep you going each and every mile.

Brake Power

Sure, speeding down a hill with a fully loaded bike is a lot of fun, but things can get down-right scary if your brakes don't work right. Check to make sure that your brakes are in order every time you board your bike. If they are not in tip-top shape, try the following:

● Clean the wheel rims with rubbing alcohol and steel wool.

● Rub the brake pads with sandpaper. This should add texture to the pads, and better texture means better gripping power.

● Check to see if your brake pads are centered and aligned with your wheel rims. Adjust if necessary.

● Take your bike into a shop for a tune-up—a bike mechanic can always help you out.

Fixing Flats

Everybody gets a flat tire once in a while, usually at the worst possible time. Fortunately, repairing flats is easy:

1. Pop the wheel off your bike.

2. Pull the tire off the rim with tire irons. This can be tricky. Slide a tire iron under the lip of the tire and pry the tire's edge over the rim. Take another tire iron and do the same thing a few inches farther down the rim. Soon you'll be able to slide the tire off the rim with your fingers or with a third tire iron.

3. Pull out the popped tube and either patch the hole or get a new tube.

4. Inspect the inside of the tire for anything sharp that might pop your new tube.

5. Pump some air into the new or repaired tube and place it on the rim beneath the lifted tire. Make sure the valve goes through the hole in the rim, and be careful not to pinch or bunch up the tube!

6. Using your fingers, push the edge of the tire back under the lip of the rim.

7. Pump up the tire, put the wheel back on your bike, and you are on your way!

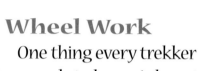

Wheel Work

One thing every trekker needs to know is how to remove a bike's wheels. If you get a flat, the wheel has to come off. If you need to squeeze your bike into a car, you may have to remove a wheel to make it fit. Want to lock your front and rear wheels together so a thief won't be tempted to steal them? You've got to take off a wheel first.

If you have a bike with quick-release wheels, the process of removing them is quite simple: Just flick open the release lever, detach the brake cable from the brake (the cable meets the brake right above the wheel), and pull the wheel out of the fork. Sometimes it's easier to get the wheels off if you turn your bike upside down.

The rear wheel is a little harder to get off than the front because you have to take the chain off first. To make it easier, just shift the chain so that it is all the way down in the lowest gear. After you undo the brake cable and the quick release, just twist and pull the wheel until it pops free of the chain.

Cooking

Planning a self-contained biking trip but have no idea what to eat or how to cook it? Relax. Cooking on the road is not that hard. With a few essential camp-kitchen appliances, a quick lesson in technique, and a shopping list, you'll be well on your way to becoming a great roadside cook. Here's what you need to know:

Stove

You need a lightweight, compact stove if you want to eat anything hot. Look for one with an adjustable flame that uses white gas. The salesperson at your local outdoors store should be able to help you find one suitable for a bike trek.

Water

As a roadside chef, you will have to drink and cook with whatever water you can find. To kill the dangerous microscopic creatures that tend to lurk in water like this, it will need to be boiled, filtered, or treated with iodine. Filters and iodine can be found at camping stores.

Pots, Pans, and Other Cooking Utensils

Good cookware for bike trekking is lightweight, easy to clean, and very compact. Look for a set that includes a pot, a pan, a cup, and a handle for gripping when pans get hot. Remember to bring utensils (fork, spoon, and a Swiss Army–style knife), a lighter, and a scouring pad for cleaning.

Packing Food

Packing is tricky. Take packaged foods out of their boxes or bags and repack in zip-locked plastic bags so your food won't spill in your panniers. Don't bring canned or bottled foods—they are too bulky and heavy.

Don't stash dried fruit at the bottom of your pannier if you are going to want to snack on it all day as you ride. Likewise, don't put dinner food near the top of your bag—you won't need it until everything is unpacked anyway. Place each meal in a separate bag to make things easy to find and to minimize sorting when it's time to cook.

Make sure anything that might spill is double-bagged and placed near the bottom of your pannier. Liquids like cooking oil should be bottled in screw-top plastic containers.

Roadside Manners

Always cook, camp, and clean at least 200 feet away from any water source. Never leave food scraps lying around camp, as they will not only attract animals but will ruin the site for the

next camper. The best way to make cleanup easy is by eating everything you cook—no leftovers.

Food Shopping

Food should be lightweight, come with minimal or no packaging, and be quick and easy to cook. Test-cook anything that you are not sure about before hitting the road. Here are some ideas:

Breakfast: Try quick-cooking oats, cereal, granola, bagels, and dried fruit (apples, banana chips, mangoes, dates, pineapples, figs, apricots, papayas, raisins). Honey adds flavor to just about any breakfast food. For liquids, bring powdered juices and energy drinks.

Lunch: Bring bread that packs easily and won't be crushed, such as pita or bagels. Peanut butter and jelly (packed in plastic squeeze bottles), cheese, and fresh vegetables are all good sandwich fillers. Dried fruit, nuts, seeds, granola, and chocolate are great for snacking, and energy bars and drinks help keep your legs moving. Your body burns a lot of calories when you go on a bike tour. It is important to make sure you get enough to eat as you go. Otherwise, you may run out of energy and not be able to continue.

Dinner: Begin with a base of rice, pasta, or any quick-cooking grain. Pack fresh vegetables such as squash, onions, and carrots. (Dried vegetables won't go bad, but they never taste as good, either.) Avoid meat, which can spoil, unless you are on a really short trip or you have a sag wagon and can keep it on ice. Remember, anything instant makes a good meal: Potatoes, sauces, and soups are a few of the options.

Preparation

Sometimes it helps to prepare food before you leave home. If you think you will be tired after a full day of pedaling, preparing ahead of time is a must. For example, if you know you will want fresh vegetables tossed into your pasta on your first night out, chop and bag them before you go.

4 Safety

Bike trekking is definitely an adventure, and it is almost always fun, but it can also be very dangerous. Loaded down with gear, you and your bike take up a significant amount of space on the road. When you are sharing that road with cars and trucks, things can get hairy. Here are a few things to keep in mind when you are "driving" your bike:

Be Predictable

Ride with traffic on the right side of the road. By moving in the same direction as the traffic, you reduce your chances of being hit. Also, always try to bike in a straight line. Never swerve into traffic and always leave a little more than a car door's width of room on your right between you and any parked cars.

Pay attention to lane markings. For example, don't go straight in a lane marked "left turn only." Obey traffic signs and signals. Not only is it dangerous to ride through stop signs and stoplights, it's also a quick way to lose the respect of drivers. Obey signs in the same way that a driver does.

Be Visible

First of all, make sure your bike is well equipped. If it's raining, snowing, or dark, you should have a strong headlight and taillight mounted on the front and back of your bike. Your bike should also include a bell and, if you have one, a rearview mirror. Reflectors on your wheels and panniers help drivers see you. You can also put reflective tape on other parts of your bike, your helmet, and on your clothing and shoes. Another good way to be seen is by wearing bright clothing. During the day, wear a bright

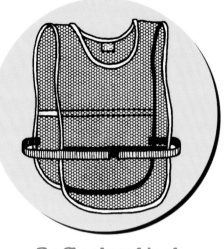

Reflector Vest

windbreaker or jersey. Some riders like to attach a tall, reflective flag to one of their rear panniers to make it even easier for drivers to see them. If you are riding at night, wear something light-colored.

Use hand signals anytime you make a move. By doing so, you are telling drivers where you are going, giving them time to avoid you. To signal a right-hand turn, either point straight out to the right with your right arm and hand, or bend your left arm at the elbow so that your left hand is straight up in the air.

Left Turn

Right Turn

To signal a left-hand turn, just point straight out to the left with your left arm and hand. You should also signal to other riders in your group any time you are going to stop. You can do this by raising an arm straight up, with your palm out, and calling out "Stopping!"

Stop

If you come to a busy intersection and want to make a left-hand turn, you have a couple of choices: You can either turn like a car or cross the intersection like a pedestrian. To turn like a car, first look to your left for traffic, signal a left-hand turn, move into the left lane, then turn left, with the flow of traffic. To cross the intersection like a pedestrian, get off your bike and walk it across the street in the crosswalk, then walk it across again to the left at the far crosswalk.

Ride Defensively

It is very important that any time you get on your bike you ride as if you are a target. This means you must always be on the defensive. Assume that no drivers can see you. Watch out for cars pulling out of driveways, switching lanes, swerving in front of you, and stopping suddenly. Try to make eye contact with a driver before you make any move to get in front of him.

It may sound like a lot of work paying attention to all the traffic in front of you and to your side, but it is even harder to watch the traffic behind you. Any time that you make a turn you must first look over your shoulder to make sure it is safe to do so. Move only when there are no vehicles in your way. This can be tricky. It is easy to lose your balance and swerve. Once you get the hang of it, though, the over-the-shoulder glance shouldn't be any problem at all.

Finally, do your best to avoid road hazards. This means constantly looking ahead for anything dangerous in the road, such as glass, rocks, bottles and cans, ice, potholes, and sewage grates. Also be careful when crossing railroad tracks, speed bumps, and curbs. If you take them at the wrong angle, you run the risk of having your whole bike—gear and all—slide out from beneath you. Ride straight at them, at a right angle, and brace yourself as you go over them.

If you have to ride on a sidewalk or if your route takes you along a bike path shared by pedestrians, always give those on foot the right of way. If you are passing someone who is on foot, warn that person first by calling out. When crossing driveways or intersections, be particularly careful that no vehicles are about to pull out.

Group Rides

Group tours require that each member of the group take certain responsibilities so that everyone can act together as a team. Communication is very important during a group ride. If you are one in a line of cyclists, you have to work together. Warn the rider behind you when you are approaching an obstacle. If you see a rock, for instance, shout "Rock!" This warning will give the cyclist behind you enough time to move to the side and avoid it.

Always ride single file. Keep several bike lengths' worth of space between you and the rider in front of you and

behind you. It takes longer to come to a complete stop when your bike is weighted down with all your trekking gear—so keep this in mind when you are riding behind someone.

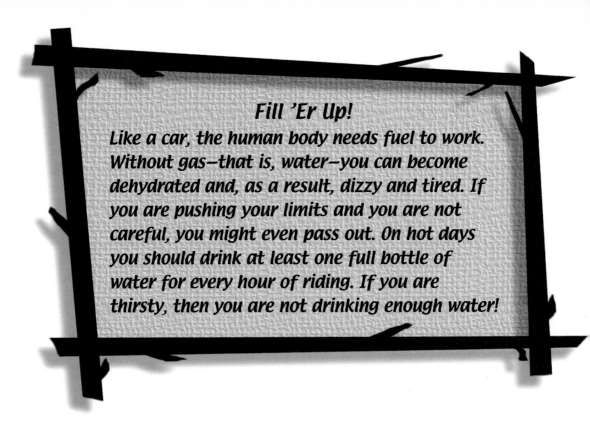

Fill 'Er Up!

Like a car, the human body needs fuel to work. Without gas—that is, water—you can become dehydrated and, as a result, dizzy and tired. If you are pushing your limits and you are not careful, you might even pass out. On hot days you should drink at least one full bottle of water for every hour of riding. If you are thirsty, then you are not drinking enough water!

Develop a system of signals and warnings. For instance, shouting "Car up!" warns the person behind you that a car is approaching in the opposite direction. "Car back!" warns all the riders ahead that a car will soon be passing on the left, in the same lane and direction. When the person nearest you calls out a warning, make sure you pass that warning on to the next rider in line.

Safe Helmets

Since 1999, bike helmets sold in the United States have had to be strong enough to satisfy the Consumer Product Safety Commission (CPSC). Look for brain buckets with the CPSC stamp of approval. If you want to be doubly sure your lid is going to protect your head in an accident, check for Snell certification as well. Snell-certified helmets are considered to be the toughest in the world.

Safety Check

It is extremely important to make sure your bike is ready to go every time you ride it. Before you start your tour, go through the following checklist:

Tires: Are they inflated to the proper pressure?

Brakes: Make sure they work. You can check the rear brake by squeezing the rear brake lever while pushing the bike forward. The rear wheel should skid. Check the front brake by doing the same thing with the front brake lever. The rear wheel should pop into the air. Make sure that the brake levers don't touch your handlebars when you squeeze them as tight as you can.

Quick releases: Check the releases on your seat and your front and rear wheels. Everything should be tight.

Lube: Lube up your chain and other moving parts. Well-lubed components are less likely to break.

Nuts and bolts: Check to make sure that nothing is loose or missing.

Helmet: Check for cracks. Make sure it fits correctly and all the straps are secure.

Wheels: Do they spin freely? Are they positioned correctly?

Other Gear: Make sure you have everything. You don't want to start out on a long trip and then realize that you forgot to pack something important.

The world of bicycle trekking is still a relatively small one. Although millions of people ride bikes, few actually use their bikes to travel long distances. For those who do trek, this is no problem—they prefer to have the roads to themselves anyway.

Most people who go on bike tours today tend to do so with an organized group under the direction of a professional touring company. By going this route they can leave the logistics—where to sleep, how many miles to ride each day, what to pack—to their guides. This is often a great way to go if you don't have riding partners or if you are just getting started and want to learn the ropes without the fear of making any mistakes. Often these tours visit sites you would otherwise miss because you had no idea they existed in the first place!

5 Bike Trekking Today

Many of today's organized tours are designed to raise awareness for certain issues—breast cancer or heart disease, for example—and to raise money. Other tours are designed strictly for fun and are organized through summer camps or local YMCAs or other youth groups. Some tours take people around the world; others just span a state or two. Some people prefer to tour alone with the elements, free to turn where they please, stop where they like, and enjoy whatever happens.

All tours, however, bring with them a sense of adventure not found in many other pursuits. The sport attracts adventurous spirits—those who prefer to take life by the reins and run rather than sit back and watch it go by. And more and more people are finding that spirit within themselves.

No, you won't be entirely alone if you decide to try bicycle trekking, but you will be different. In a world of cars, planes, and high technology, pedal power is perceived as a throwback to the old days—a time when people had to use their legs to get where they wanted to go.

Try bike trekking. You just might find that life on two wheels, slow as it might seem, is worth the time and effort.

Over the Great Divide

If you've got a mountain bike, some trekking experience, and an urge for serious adventure, a bike trip down the Great Divide may be just what you need. The mostly off-road Great Divide mountain bike route, established and mapped by the Adventure Cycling Association, cuts a path from the Canada-Montana border over the steep passes of the southern Colorado Rockies and through the high desert of New Mexico. The route often climbs to elevations greater than 10,000 feet.

Although there are many things Great Divide trekkers must do to prepare for this three-month cross-country trip, gaining an understanding of the mountains and how they will affect your trip is perhaps the most important. An extended tour at high altitudes—greater than 8,000 feet above sea level—can be extremely challenging. At high altitudes, the body simply does not work the same way it does at lower elevations. Staying hydrated becomes extremely important. You

have to change clothes almost as often as you change gears. And the weather can be perfect ... or terrible.

The Great Divide route's creator, Michael McCoy, recommends riding the route from north to south and beginning

Club Ped

If you are looking for riding partners, one of the best ways to find some is by joining or starting a touring club. Ask the folks at your local bike shop if there is already an established club in your area. If not, put up notices in the shop and on other community boards advertising your club's first meeting. You are bound to make a bunch of new trekker friends.

in early July. By starting in the summer, you can avoid the heavy snow in the high mountains of the southern Colorado Rockies. And New Mexico—the high-desert part of the trip—can be biked in the fall, when the temperature is perfect for cycling.

Nevertheless, starting in July doesn't ensure that everything will go smoothly. The route commonly features three types of weather that can be dangerous for the unprepared rider. The first is rainstorms. You can expect rough conditions along many parts of the route if it gets wet.

"It can get real slick and impassable when you get into rainy periods," says McCoy. "The mud cakes up so badly in your tires that you can't go anywhere." But there is a solution: "Always carry a day or two of extra food in case you have to hole up for a while," McCoy says.

The second weather danger is cold. Cold rain, wind, and snow can occur at any time, even in the summer. "It might be 90 degrees when you set out from some valley town in Colorado," says McCoy, "but on the same day you can run into dangerously cold weather conditions up high." To avoid serious problems, pack your panniers with warm clothing and lots of food and water.

Finally, trekkers need to beware of lightning. Dark thunderclouds are very common on summer afternoons at a high altitude. "You might be caught in a thunderstorm while two miles away the sun is still shining," says McCoy. If you're caught in a storm, stay away from tall trees and crouch close

to the ground in a low area. Try sitting on your panniers, keeping your body, especially your feet, off the ground.

Other Tips

The following tips apply not only to cycling the Great Divide but to just about any bike trek through the mountains. In fact, they constitute good advice for any kind of bike trekking—or any type of outdoor activity, for that matter.

Pack Carefully. Be prepared for anything the mountains may throw your way, including rain, hail, snow, sleet, fog, lightning, high winds, intense sunshine, and bitter cold. At 8,000 feet of elevation, whether you are in New Mexico, Colorado, Wyoming, or Montana, it can be very hot during the day and freezing at night. Storms can come in fast—if you see scary-looking clouds, find shelter immediately. Don't forget to pack carefully. Fill those panniers with essentials like warm fleece, windproof and waterproof jacket and pants, hat and gloves, and extra food and water.

Be Self-Sufficient. You may be far from help when things go wrong. Know what to do in an emergency. Carry a first-aid kit and learn CPR (cardiopulmonary resuscitation) and basic first aid before you leave home.

Listen to Your Body. It can be hard to breathe at high altitudes. Your body, which needs oxygen, has more and more trouble getting the necessary amount the higher you climb above sea level. Your body has to acclimatize—get used to the thin air. While it does, you must take it easy. Once you are acclimatized, you will find that the cycling gets a lot easier.

Water and Food. It is easy to get dehydrated at high altitudes. Drink as much water as you can. Your body also needs more calories to make up for the extra energy it takes to push your pedals, so eat up.

The Environment. Stay on the trail. Practice "Leave No Trace" camping and leave the trail and the scenery in the same shape that you found it.

Leave No Trace

Bicycle tourists have a lot to think about, from what to pack to where to go. But one thing many people forget is that it is equally important to make sure your trek does nothing to harm the environment. Littering, riding off the road or trail, and camping in fragile natural areas all can hurt the land that you have boarded your bike to see. Practice the following six Leave No Trace principles every time you go on a tour and do your part to save the environment.

1. *Plan ahead and prepare.* Know where you're going, how to get there, and what you will need to make the trip.

2. *Travel and camp on durable surfaces.* Don't ride or camp on anything that can't handle your bike or tent!

3. *Leave nothing behind.* Pack out everything you pack in, including food scraps, trash, and toilet paper. If you can't find a trash can, pack it away and hold on to it until later.

4. *Properly dispose of what you can't pack out. **And always bury your waste!***

5. *Leave what you find the same way that you found it. **Everything has its place. Leave things for others to enjoy.***

6. *Minimize the use and impact of fire. **If you have to make a campfire, be careful not to leave any sign of it once it is out.***

For more information, contact the national Leave No Trace organization at (800) 332-4100, or visit their Web site at http://www.lnt.org.

Tour Guide

Want to trek with an organized group? Check out the Web site of the National Bicycle Tour Directors Association, *http://www.okfreewheel.com/nbtda.html*. This collection of bicycle-ride coordinators and directors maintains a list of organized multi-day rides in North America. Just scan the calendar for a tour near you, jot down the appropriate contact information, and you'll be on your way.

Breathe a Little Easier

If you're interested in trekking for a good cause, the American Lung Association (ALA) could use your help. The ALA, a national organization that works to combat lung diseases such as asthma, emphysema, and cancer, sponsors many health programs, fundraisers, and special events around the country. One of these events is the annual Big Ride Across America.

The Big Ride is a forty-eight-day, 3,250-mile, fully supported bicycle trek from Seattle, Washington, to Washington, DC. As participants pedal across America's heartland, they raise money and awareness for the ALA's fight against lung disease.

For all the details, go to the Big Ride Web page at *http://www.bigride.com*, or e-mail the American Lung Association at *bigride@lungusa.org*, or call (877) BIG-RIDE. And don't worry if this trek sounds as if it may be too long for you. The ALA also sponsors many shorter bicycling events. Give your local branch of the ALA a call at (800) LUNG-USA.

Glossary

Bonk
To become so tired that you can't ride anymore.

Fire Road
A dirt mountain road wide enough for a truck.

Granny Gear
The easiest gear on a bike, used for climbing steep hills.

Lube
Oil or grease used to lubricate bike components.

Panniers
Bags that can be attached to the frame of a bike. Think of them as suitcases for your bicycle tour.

Rig
Slang for a bike.

Sag Wagon
A support vehicle.

Singletrack
A trail wide enough for one rider.

Snakebite

A flat tire caused by hitting an obstacle so hard that the inner tube pinches against the wheel rim. The resulting tube puncture resembles two fang holes.

Spin

To pedal with smooth, fast, efficient strokes.

Washboard

Soil ripples on a trail that make riding very bumpy.

Washout

A water-eroded area on a trail.

Resources

Web Sites

There are hundreds of Web sites devoted to cycling, camping, gear, and the outdoors in general. In addition, there are a few sites devoted specifically to bicycle touring. Surf the Net and see what you can find! Here are a few sites to get you started:

Bicycle Online
http://www.bicycle.com

Bicycle Touring
http://www.users.aol.com/btouring/home.htm

Bicycling Magazine
http://www.bicyclingmagazine.com

Bikealog
http://www.bikealog.com

Bike Ride Online
http://www.bikeride.com

Bikeshops Online
http://www.bikeshops.com

Cyber Cyclery
http://www.cyclery.com

Gearhead Magazine
http://www.gearhead.com

Great Outdoors
http://www.greatoutdoors.com

International Cycling Union
http://www.uci.ch

Interzine
http://www.ibike.com

Mountain Zone
http://www.mountainzone.com

Organizations

Adventure Cycling Association
P.O. Box 8308
Missoula, MO 59807
(800) 755-2453
e-mail: acabike@adv-cycling.org
Web site: http://www.adv-cycling.org

American Camping Association
5000 State Road, #67
North Martinsville, IN 46151-7902
(800) 428-CAMP
Web site: http://www.acacamps.org

American Youth Hostels (AYH)
P.O. Box 37613
Washington, DC 20013-7613
(202) 783-6161
Web site: http: //www.hiayh.org

Bicycle Federation of America (BFA)
1818 R Street NW
Washington, DC 20009
(202) 332-6986
Web site: http:// bfa@igc.org

International Mountain Bicycling Association (IMBA)
P.O. Box 7578
Boulder, CO 80306
(303) 545-9011
e-mail: imba@aol.com
Web site: http://www.imba.com

League of American Bicyclists
1612 K Street NW, Suite 401
Washington, DC 20006
(202) 822-1333
e-mail: bikeleague@bikeleague.org
Web site: http://www.bikeleague.org,

National Highway Traffic Safety Administration
Safety Countermeasures Division
400 Seventh Street SW NTS 23
Washington, DC 20590
(202) 366-1739

National Off-Road Bicycle Association (NORBA)
One Olympic Plaza
Colorado Springs, CO 80909
(719) 578-4581
Web site: http://www.usacycling.org/mtb

For Further Reading

Books

Editors of *Bicycling* Magazine. *Bicycling Magazine's Bicycle Touring in the '90s.* Emmaus, PA: Rodale Press, 1993.

Lovett, Richard A. *The Essential Touring Cyclist: A Complete Course for the Bicycle Traveler.* Camden, ME: Rugged Mountain Press, 1994.

Oliver, Peter. *Bicycling: Touring and Mountain Bike Basics.* New York: W. W. Norton, 1996.

Smith, John. *Cycling the USA: Bicycle Touring Nationwide.* Osceola, WI: Motorbooks International, 1997.

U.S. Olympic Committee (Richard D. Burns, ed.). *A Basic Guide to Cycling.* Glendale, CA: Griffin Publishing Group, 1997.

Van der Plas, Rob. *The Bicycle Touring Manual: Using the Bicycle for Touring and Camping.* Osceola, WI: Motorbooks International, 1997.

Magazines

Adventure Cyclist
Adventure Cycling Association
P.O. Box 8308
Missoula, MT 59807
(406) 721-1776
e-mail: acabike@aol.com
Web site: http://www.adv-cycling.org

Bicycling
Box 7308
Red Oak, IA 51591-0308
(800) 666-2806
e-mail: BicMagDM@aol.com;
Web site: http://www.bicyclingmagazine.com

Bike
Box 1028
Dana Point, CA 92629
(800) 765-5501
e-mail: bikemag@petersenpub.com

VeloNews
1830 North 55th Street
Boulder, CO 80301
(303) 440-0601
e-mail: vninteractive@7dogs.com;
Web site: http://www.velonews.com

Index

Credits

About the Author
Chris Hayhurst is a freelance journalist living in northern Colorado. He is the author of several books for young readers.

Photo Credits
Cover photo ©Anne Marie Weber/Mountain Stock; p. 5 © Bud Fawcett /MountainStock; pp. 8, 15, 30 by Thaddeus Harden; p. 9, 50 ©Anne Marie Weber/Mountain Stock; pp. 11, 41 Associated Press AP; p. 12 © Bob Firth/International Stock Inc.; pp. 19, 29 © Michael Lanza; pp. 25, 26, 33 © AllSport Photography; p. 28 © Jim Sugar Photography/CORBIS; pp. 34, 49, 53 © Bob Woodward/ Mountain Stock; p. 35 © Phil Schermeister/CORBIS; p. 45 © Vandystadt/ Allsport France; p. 47 © Associated Press, Tanqueray; p. 55 © Scott Barrow/ International Stock.

Series Design
Oliver Rosenberg

Layout
Laura Murawski

DATE DUE

4-2-09